MW00886487

A Spiral Wind

A Spiral Wind

Poems by Burt Porter

iUniverse, Inc.
New York Lincoln Shanghai

A Spiral Wind

Copyright © 2005 by Burt Porter

iUniverse books may be ordered through booksellers or by contacting:

iUniverse
2021 Pine Lake Road, Suite 100
Lincoln, NE 68512
www.iuniverse.com
1-800-Authors (1-800-288-4677)

Cover art: steel sculpture "The Green Man" by Torin Porter
Photo by Torin Porter

ISBN-13: 978-0-595-35990-5 (pbk)
ISBN-13: 978-0-595-80441-2 (ebk)
ISBN-10: 0-595-35990-6 (pbk)
ISBN-10: 0-595-80441-1 (ebk)

Printed in the United States of America

To my family and friends, with special thanks to Torin Porter, Lindsay Knowlton and Lee Webster for invaluable editing.

The Green Man

Stepping slowly from the trees,
The Green Man dances with the wind,
In a circle like the sky
For where he ends all things begin.

The Green Man dances on the hill,
He dances East, North, West, and South,
Swaying branches are his limbs;
Flowers blossom from his mouth.

Through the Summer sun and rain
In a circle like the sky,
The Green Man dances on the hill;
When Winter comes then he must die.

When the Winter's wind shall blow
The last leaves from the bare, dark trees,
The Green Man's hair will fill with snow
And his bright green blood will freeze.

Ice and snow shall freeze his heart,
Cold and stiff his limbs and eyes,
When springtime melts the ice and snow,
The Green Man once again shall rise.

Stepping slowly from the trees
The Green Man dances with the wind,
In a circle like the sky
For where he ends all things begin.

Contents

The Natural World

Family and Friends

Love

Humanities

From the Homeric World

Acknowledgements

Several poems have previously appeared in various publications:

Hellas—"Modesty"

The Formalist—"Unequal Tender", "Cassandra", "Zeus", "Homer", and "Hawk-Owl"

The Classical Outlook—"Penelope", "Odysseus at 90 Remembers the Princess Nausicäa", "Circe", and "Diomedes Speaks of Fame"

Poet—"Two Buildings"

Blue Unicorn—"Early Summer Rain", "A Girl Reading the Iliad", and "Night Song"

Snowy Egret—"Tracking Lessons"

The Lyric—"Janus", "Milkweed", "Preaching to the Birds" (Best of Issue Prize, Winter 1997), "Three Birds" (published separately in three issues), "Natural Order" and "Old Poems"

The Green Mountain Trading Post—"Hawk Dance", "Rainbow", "Putting in the Peas", "Editing", "The Last of Autumn", "Killing Time", and "Finding One's Way"

Magnetic North—"Geese in October"

Dog Pond Review—"The Day My Father Climbed to Heaven"

The Frog Peak Anthology—"Falling Dream"

Lambs and Trochees—"Eyes" and "Words for the Ghost"

The Natural World

A Seasonal Sequence

I

The frost-ferns on the frozen windowpane
Grow quickly in the silent winter night—
At dawn we find them there. Who could explain
How water dreams these forms or by what sleight
The graceful fronds appear? And as we dream
In the long stillness of the winter night
And breath drifts from our sleeping mouths like steam,
Into our minds come pictures, clear and bright,
Of things that we have surely never seen—
Angelic beings, gleaming like the light
Of dawn that fills the frosted windowpane
With burning red and pink and glowing white.
    Such shapes spring forth unasked for our delight
    In the long, cold, and silent winter night.

II

Reluctantly the winter snows melt down—
Even in the pale green glow of May
High on northern slopes, on shaded ground,
A few tenacious hard-packed drifts still stay,
And in the gullies where the streams run down
Among dark spruce, where not the sharpest ray
Of sun can stab the shade, ice can be found
That will not quickly melt and run away.
And I have had my inner storms and snows
And all too long the icy drifts remain—
Sometimes it seems that what the winter froze

Could never thaw and come to life again,
But soon the sun will trim away the night
And melt the ice and fill the world with light.

III

A little while each year, the summer sun
Shines down on these cold hills, and every leaf
Seeks what it can until the season's done—
Lord knows the summertime is all too brief.
I walk through fields of tasseled corn and smell
The heavy, warm, sweet scent. I cut a stem
From a pumpkin vine and make a horn to call
Wild, unknown beasts. What is this sound to them?
But soon enough the autumn winds will blow
The frosted, many-colored leaves away,
And once again far-calling geese will go,
And once again I know that I will stay;
Let us store up what we can together
In these short weeks of easy summer weather.

IV

Now corn stalks rattle in the autumn wind
And frost has filled the air with sharp new smells
Of ferment. Wild apples make the branches bend
And empty milkweed pods like dry conch shells
Murmur of a season laid to rest.
Migrant flocks rustle in the bright hedgerows
Where berries fall in an abandoned nest.
From far off comes the lonely sound of crows,
Caustic comments on the passing fall.
At dawn, between the hills, the fog lies low,

Solid, as if the vapor could recall
Glaciers that filled the valleys long ago,
    And soon enough a colder wind will blow
    And fill the brown, dry fields with drifting snow.

Spring: Theory and Practice

The weathermen say Spring's begun.
The earth has spun around the sun
To the point marked on its orbit's bend
That says we've come to Winter's end—
Yet snow falls thick and hard and fast.
Although it likely will not last,
We've seen enough to have good reason
To doubt there's been a change of season.
What Science says often denies
What's right there before our eyes;
The notion that the earth spins 'round
Would have us clinging to the ground,
But that for practical intents
We just rely on common sense.

Early Spring

From the birch beside the barn
The blue jay's liquid call denotes
A day in March so bright and warm
That heavy woolen winter coats
Once tightly buttoned to our throats
Hang open in the easy breeze
While 'round the house the chickadees
Whistle now their clear "phoebe's",
Then fly to the porch and scold for seeds
(Sunflower only, if you please).

The wind blows with a softer sound
And here and there we see bare ground,
A sight we scarcely can recall—
We haven't seen such since last fall.
Though winter isn't quite yet done,
The water dripping in the sun
Sparkles with a promise bright
Of the dawning end of winter's night.

Morning Dew

The morning dew is silver on the lawn
Save for two lines, dark and green, that show
Where I walked to hear the robin's song
And fetch some lovage and oregano.
The morning dew will soon enough be gone;
There is no way to make this moment last
Or keep the lines I wrote upon the grass
Except to make these words into a poem,
Scarcely more enduring than the two
Faint lines now fading with the morning dew;
Little that a mortal man has done
Will last until that far off, final dawn.

April First

Now as we watch the snow retreat
We estimate how many feet
Of brown and flattened April field
By melting snow has been revealed.
Dank, bleared ground, long in the dark
Beneath the drifts still bears the mark
Of tons of deep-packed, sodden snow—
So on this land the marks still show
Of massive glaciers, long ago.

Soon on this field the dandelions
Will glow like twenty thousand suns
And in a world of green and gold
We will forget the winter's cold,
As in this world of gold and green
With blossoms like a May-day queen
We frolic in the time between
The last and next Pleistocene.

Hawk Dance

Warmed by the early April sun,
I sat against a smooth gray stone
On grass that still lay pressed down flat.
Although the heavy snow was gone.
The sun shone bright; I tipped my hat
And gazed at a narrowed band of sky,
Then on the lilting April wind
A broad-winged hawk came soaring by.
I watched him as he dipped and rose,
Marking the cresting waves of air,
Then from behind my hat's dark brim
Five more hawks came wheeling there.
Behind my head, the earth was turning;
The hawks above went 'round and 'round
In stately grace, a formal dance
To wind-blown music with no sound.
Sometimes they would pair off and two
Would soar together, wing to wing,
Then all would join and move as one
Like carol dancers in a ring.
And so they drifted on the wind
And spiraled off across the sky
Until they vanished in the air
Like motes that drift across the eye.
The ponderous stone behind my head,
The matted grass, the weeds and stalks
Were waiting there when I came back
From wandering with six broad-winged hawks.

The Half-Moon

The pale half-moon in early May half-light
Has risen from the hill where poplars glow
Soft yellow green like pastel mist, bright
Against dark, pointed spruce that still hide snow.
From the new-thawed marsh the peep frogs sound
Their endless song, and all the gentle air
Smells of new-mown grass and new-plowed ground
And green things sprouting, budding everywhere.
I walk up through the orchard to the hill
And watch the plovers in their wheeling flight
Until the air turns damp and cool and still
And twilight slowly darkens into night,
    And now the pale half-moon is climbing high
    In the vastness of the dark, indifferent sky.

Snow in Late May

The daffodils have all gone by;
The tulips bring their blossoms forth,
Yet snow falls from the heavy sky
And cold winds come from the far North.

Upon the porch the bright spring birds
Seek the seed we scatter there
And if their songs had any words
They'd ask to flutter in warmer air.

Then through the slanting swirls of snow
Comes a darting, crimson streak,
A hummingbird with throat aglow,
A blur of wings and slender beak,

Come all the way from Mexico
To find our flowers in the snow.

Putting in the Peas

I rake the dark, deep-tilled soil
To make the bed smooth and flat,
Then fetch the pale, round, wrinkled peas
That I carried up in my hat,
And scatter them out at random
Like stars, flung from a mighty hand,
And call it a cosmic pattern
Wherever they happen to land.
Wait till they send up thrusting sprouts
Then give them a fence to climb
Ever nearer to heaven
Until it's blossom time.
When the new peas grow fat and sweet
And swell each curving pod,
I'll be back to harvest all
Like some barbarous god.

Editing

I coat the corn seeds with tar
To keep away the crows,
Then plant them close together
In more or less straight rows.

In a week or so come the little sprouts
Like rough lines of sharp green nails,
Driven up through the crusted soil
By a force that seldom fails.

Soon each sprout grows a pair of leaves
Like arms lifted up in praise,
Dancing in exultation—
So it seems on windy days,

Which is why I wait for calmer air
Before I take my hoe
And cut down all the weakest plants
And those that crowd the row.

Early Summer Rain

The summer evening's gently falling rain
Turns the well-tilled garden nearly black
And brings to sprout the newly planted grain
And coats the pale green, slender tamarack
With silver drops hung from each needle's end,
And where the dark and pointed spruces stand,
Great swirling masses of gray clouds descend
To form a curtain hung across the land.
And when the rain clouds slowly drift away
The last song of the evening hermit thrush
Ripples in the quiet close of day
And leaves the evening in a breathless hush,
    And here and there a firefly shines bright
    Beneath the distant stars, so few this night.

The Lake and the Sky

Above the lake the naked cliffs ascend
Towards the bright, cloud-scattered summer sky
Where wild-eyed falcons ride the twisting wind.
Looking downward through a falcon's eye,
One sees a woman, naked on the sand,
Arise and step into the lake and there
She stoops to take clear water in her hand
And lets it flow upon her face and hair.
The spattered water dimples at her knees;
She dives, then floats at ease upon her back,
And up against the high, white clouds she sees
A falcon, to her eye a tiny speck;
    She watches as he wheels and soars so high
    Above the lake, brim-full of summer sky.

Dandelions

Like sparkles on a green and windblown sea
Or stars, scattered in a deep green sky,
The dandelions blossom in the field
In constellations to bemuse the eye.
As distant stars become the Milky Way,
Further off the flowers merge into
A gleaming galaxy, a massed display
Of solid gold beneath the sky's bright blue.
The blossoms soon will shrink to buds again,
Then bloom once more as soft, white, fragile spheres
That burst their seeds to ride upon the wind
To meadows that are far away from here.
    Like silent songs, the seeds drift in the air
    And take root where they can, most anywhere.

Rainbow

Dark clouds surged up from behind the hills;
Across the valley we could see
Gray drifting shrouds of ghostly rain
And lightning streaking crookedly.
Then the thunder crashed, we ran for home
To look out as for miles around
The wind blew out of a sky gone mad
And fire and water shook the ground.

Then we stepped out into a field
Where all the grass lay battered down
To see a spectrum of pure light
Arcing high above the sodden ground.
As if the ever-faithful sun
Hung colors in the tender air
To tell us that the sun, like love,
Though masked by clouds, is always there.

Milkweed

I watched a white-winged seed ascend
On an unsteady breeze,
Until it spun up out of sight
Above the empty trees.

When the snows came drifting down
Such whiteness from on high
Made me think that I had seen
A milkweed sow the sky.

Fog and Flares

On an early morn in May
The morning fog lay thick and low;
Old trees that stood not far away
Their tall, dark shapes did scarcely show.
Scattered on the nearby slope
Across the dooryard, below the hill
Was a fleet of daffodils
Like gleaming yellow periscopes
Peering up from bulbs below
To check for some last trace of snow,
Each glowing like a yellow flare
Through the gray and heavy air.
Then came a bright and golden finch
To settle on a bending branch;
The sunlight spread across the lawn
And soon the morning fog was gone.

Killing Time

As the last of the twilight faded away,
I lay back in the new-mown hay
And sang old ballads to the sky;
A summer's day is slow to die.

The field mice scurried here and there
Between the windrows in stubble bare
And the cat had come up from the house
To have an evening meal of mouse.

The light was fading; when I tried
To see the cat, I looked aside
From where he sat and let him be
Blurred in my periphery.

The last of light was all but gone
And with the dark the dew came on.
I slowly rose and stepped away;
I called the cat, but he would stay.

Then from the black woods up the hill
Came cries of coyotes at the kill
Eerie, yipping, yapping sounds
As might come from the Devil's hounds.

So I turned back; the cat now thought
That he'd best let himself be caught.
I picked him up and left the field
To what the night had now concealed.

Three Birds

Great Blue Heron

He seems to swim through easy air,
His wings flap slow, a steady pair
Of fins that float him in the dusk
Above the swampland sedge and brush.
From some far distant time he seems,
A time we remember from old dreams,
And when he's gone behind the hill,
The marsh is empty, calm and still.

Raven

Somewhere in the snow-filled sky
A raven calls his hollow cry
Of cold and wind and gray half-light
That quickly darkens into night.

Crow

The rumpled crow, tumbled and tossed,
Flaps and regains the span he lost:
Against the flow of night and day
The mind makes its uncertain way.

Natural Order

In the early summer's morn, the brisk red hen
Is methodically pecking at the addled head
Of a white chick that strayed into her pen;
She holds him with her foot until he's dead.
Indoors, the kitchen radio recites
The daily catalog of gruesome news
Of slaughter, and denial of those rights
That Jefferson declared no man could lose.
Meanwhile, out in the garden, life goes on,
The same, but slower. There the bindweed takes
All day to lunge at the unwary corn,
Strangling the stalks like green, lethargic snakes.
    Back in the house, draining water flows
    In counterclockwise swirl. And so it goes.

The Snow Goose

"Oh, do not shoot the snow goose
For snow geese are so few!"
"I see broad gaggles cross the skies
As they go passing through."

"But do not shoot the snow goose
For I'm told they mate for life!"
"Then why not shoot the gander
If I also shoot his wife?"

"But if you shoot the snow goose,
Then I fear my heart should break,
So you must spare the snow goose
If only for my sake."

"Look yonder where the snow goose
Squawks into the skies—
I will spare the snow goose
To keep sorrow from your eyes."

The Killing Frost

The night was cold, clear and still;
The stars were close; the moon was full;
Dark leaves at sunrise told the cost;
The last of the harvest we had lost.

Then crystals by the sun were burned
To smoky mist; leaves slowly turned
And spun to float as in a dream
On the dark, clear waters of the pasture stream.

Inspiration

The silence of the autumn woods
Was breathless as a still, clear pond;
No slight breeze rustled the dry leaves;
No crows called from the hills beyond.

Nor I nor any thing had moved
For so long it began to seem
As if the sun itself were stopped
And standing still, as in a dream.

Amid a bed of fragile fern
One frond began to tremble there
And then danced wildly in the sway
Of an idle whim of idle air

That touched no other of the ferns;
All about the bracken stood
As still as if time still were stopped
There in the silent autumn wood.

Then a flock of raucous jays
Quarreled in the distant trees;
A red squirrel scolded, and the leaves
Began to rustle in the breeze.

The sun moved on; the shadow grew
From the rising westward hill
And I moved on, remembering
The fern that danced when all was still.

Geese in October

Always first I hear their calls—
Like swirling snow, their yelping cries
Drift over cold and bleak brown hills
Down through cold and bleak gray skies
Like sifted sounds that seem to come
From nowhere and from everywhere.
Then I see the arrowing gaggles
Following pathways in the air
Harbingers of the winter's weather—
With head thrown back, I stand and stare.

They call me, though, to no long journey;
Here I am and here I stay,
Glad to stand beside my woodpile
As I watch them go their way.

A Spiral Wind

It was a yellow autumn.
The slow oncoming cold
Had turned but few leaves scarlet;
The rest were mostly gold,

And on a bright October day
The sunlight gleaming through
The hardwoods made a golden glow
As when the world was new.

Beneath a tree a spiral wind
Arose to pluck it bare,
And glittering golden leaves spun up
In the bright October air.

They flashed and sparkled in the sun,
Then rose beyond our sight,
Fading like the last small stars
That leave with the morning light.

Should they ever return to Earth
To blacken into mold,
In time they will arise again
And turn again to gold,

Or should they keep on spinning up
Past Venus or past Mars,
The golden leaves will find a place
Among the spiraling stars.

Old Growth Maples

The twinned seeds of the maple tree have wings
But cannot really fly—they only spin
A little while upon the wind that brings
Them down, close to their tree of origin.
Each year, thousands of spinners swirl from each
Old tree, enough to start the forest new;
Only a few will sprout and try to reach
Life-giving light before the others do.
The saplings struggle, there in the dappled shade,
Straggling always upwards, spindly and lean,
Until they crowd the light within the glade
And die beneath the canopy of green,
>And when the old tree falls and leaves a space,
>Only one young tree can take its place.

The best genetics give no guarantee
Which seed will grow to flourish in the sun
And cast in time its windblown legacy
In whirling script against oblivion.
The strongest seeds may land on hostile stone
Or float a while in pools 'til they decay;
Where they may land is where they may be blown
By winds that care not where small seeds may stray.
Beneath the wheeling sun and shifting moon,
The years turn and the spinning seeds swirl down;
The old tree smothers seedlings born too soon—
The late-born die beneath the new tree's crown.
>Blind chance, not strength alone, decides which tree
>Survives of Nature's great fecundity.

Yet from this chaos comes a kind of grace:
The soaring trunks, the great limbs' upward arc
Above gray lichens growing soft as lace
Spread upon the dark and creviced bark,
The glory of the dying leaves in fall,
Frostbitten into colored majesty,
Careless beauty that has no use at all,
Beauty that is ours alone to see.
We too have struggled upwards toward the light
And over-shadowed others along the way
To stay somehow alive as best we might
And walk among the trees another day
    To know the loveliness that struggle breeds
    And see the spinning of the maple seeds.

The Last of Autumn

Now are the last bright, easy Autumn days
Before the long, hard winter settles in,
When in late afternoons a smoky haze
Settles in the swale, and birds begin
To gather in great wheeling flocks that turn
In unison, as if their thoughts were part
Of some far greater mind; as if they learn
It all while in the egg—an innate art.
Then darkness wraps us like a wizard's cloak,
Close and bat-winged, thick with mystery;
Breath lingers long in clouds of pale gray smoke;
We go indoors to firelight and tea.
    Catlike, the night purrs 'round the house and then
    Rubs against the frosted windowpane.

The Partridge

As I drove past an orchard,
Abandoned long ago,
The air was bright with autumn light
And autumn's orange glow.

A partridge flew out from the brush;
I felt him strike the car;
I stopped, walked back and looked for him;
He hadn't gone that far.

He lay there in the colored leaves
Of maple, ash and oak,
And never twitched a feather;
His dark ruffed neck had broke.

I wondered what had made him fly
So recklessly that day,
To meet his death out on the road
In such a random way.

I opened my knife and dressed him out;
His crop was tightly filled
With pieces pecked from apples.
Their juice had got him killed.

And when I breathed their fragrance
Like fermented apple wine,
I too was drunk with autumn
And autumn apple time.

Mars

When Mars came close, we stood and gazed
Up at the planet that rose each night
In the south-southeast where it loomed and blazed,
A blood-red orb, an ominous sight.

The last time Mars came around this near,
Old Stone Age hunters watched the sky
And donned the antlers and skins of deer
And drummed and danced and knew not why.

Now we can chart each planet's course,
Predict their movements in the sky
And trace the universe to its source
With theories we almost verify.

Yet all we know cannot subdue
The ancient, savage hearts of men;
What drums will we be dancing to
When Mars comes back this way again?

Tracking Lessons

Out in the woods you only rarely see
A perfect track, printed in bare, damp soil;
You learn to go by patterns of disturbance.
No slightly displaced leaf alone can tell
The line of travel, but dozens of such signs
Can spell a story in the littered mold.

Don't think in words; slow down, listen,
Be aware of shifts of wind, of scents
You barely smell, of cries of distant jays.
Be watchful, but do not force your eyes to see,
Rather, learn to let your eyes go slack
And at the shifting, shadowed periphery
Signs so faint you could not find just one
Will form a path that shows where you must follow.

Look for nibbled twigs, broken bark,
Middens of shucked shells, piles of scat
(Break them apart and look for tiny fragments
of what was eaten). Then get down on all fours,
Crawl quietly over rough ground; look
Through animal eyes, think animal thoughts;
Be wary; feel the danger and the joy.

And when you come to where the trodden ferns
Are nodding slowly upright and a presence
Wraps around you like a silent wind,
Breathe deep and slow, inhale that primal musk
Into your lungs, into your feral blood
And whatever you have found you will become.

The Watchers

They watch and wait, somewhere up there,
Soaring easy, circling high,
Floating on currents of rising air,
Unseen against the bright, hard sky.

They watch us all that live below
Waiting for the time when we
Lurch and stagger—down we go;
They wait for us most patiently.

At intervals determined by
How far a vulture's eye can see
They hover, spread across the sky,
And watch each other endlessly.

Those lines of sight then act like strings;
When one drops lower as something dies
The others wheel on wide, curved wings
To follow where the first one flies.

And when at last they swarm upon
The carcass of whatever dies
They gorge until they barely can
Lumber aloft into the skies.

Geese at the Solstice

The year turned and the solstice neared;
The sun was weak, the sun was low;
December light fell listlessly
On hills and fields all bare of snow,
And still at noon it seemed half-night
With no snow to enhance the light.

And then the wind brought Winter on—
At dawning of the shortest day
The first white flakes came spinning down;
The air turned cold, the sky turned gray
And as the clouds came thick and low
The hills and fields turned white with snow.

Falling mingled with the flakes
Came gabbling, yelping, lonely cries
Of geese who fled the freezing land
Flying through the snow-filled skies.
That night the moon made a pale glow
Through the clouds and falling snow.

Gyrfalcon

A white expanse of snow-filled field
Below a gray and snow-filled sky,
Fine, ice-hard, wind-blown flakes
To sting the face and sting the eye—

The blank, white field, the swirling snow
Held the eye and mind spell-bound
Until there seemed no way to tell
Whirling sky from whirling ground.

As if born forth from sky and snow
A gray-and-white gyrfalcon came
And hunted over the empty field
In search of soft, warm, twitching game,

Then flew off onward to the North
To merge once more with snow and sky—
The air felt empty, yet alive,
As if some god had just passed by.

Hawk-Owl

The frozen bog lies silent, white and black;
A few fine flakes of snow sift slowly down
On stunted spruce and wind-torn tamarack
As gray light fades and night comes early on.

Atop the tallest of the broken trees,
The northern hawk-owl watches where below,
Beneath the briars and the brush, he sees
A telltale sudden scurry in the snow.

He launches on a breeze as soft as breath;
His wings caress the currents of the air;
He comes, a floating specter of gray death;
He tears and eats the flesh, the bones and hair,

Then back up to his chosen tree he flies
To stare upon the swamp with golden eyes.

Nightsong

Sometimes in the night I hear them call;
When the moon is bright enough that shadows
Of trees, reaching dark, long-branched and tall,
Fall sharply etched across the level snow,
The wolves then howl their ancient eulogy,
And I pull on my pants and boots and coat
And go out on the hill to hear their harmony
And feel the tug of song within my throat.
My blood grows thick, my jaw hangs agape,
I shudder and grunt, my pulse pounds strong and slow,
And now within my mouth the song takes shape
And rings out as it did a million years ago,
    Echoing through the turning zodiac;
    From far across the hills the wolves howl back.

A Falling Leaf

A yellow leaf, dry enough to drift
A while on air, spun slowly down,
Slipping this way and that, as if
Reluctant to touch the steadfast ground.

The lines that leaf sketched in the air
Will likely never be drawn again,
Nor ever likely were drawn before,
Only now, and never then.

Countless times this spinning sphere
Has wobbled its way around the sun,
Every orbit another year
That's been rolled out, rolled up and done.

Never a leaf, yellow and dry,
Has fallen as this one slowly spun,
In all the years that have passed by,
In all the years that yet may come.

Pumpkins

In autumn when the frost has killed
The leaves and vines so they die down,
Then one can see the fields are filled
With pumpkins scattered on the ground.

And then they're gathered and heaped high
In glowing piles beside the road
To the delight of passersby,
And soon enough they're mostly sold.

Some will go to pumpkin pies
And some will go to pumpkin bread
But most will get a mouth and eyes
To scare away what we may dread.

Now only used for food in part,
A kind of agricultural art,
Pumpkins are grown for what they mean
On Thanksgiving and Halloween.

Family and Friends

Remnants

My grandfather died when I was small;
I don't remember him much at all.
Some drawings, some photos, a clock he made,
Some letters, some echoes of things he said,
A fine old fiddle and a fine old bow
Are pretty much all the little I know
Of a man who's been gone since I was small—
I don't remember him much at all.

Of all the things he did and could do,
The things he said and the music he knew,
The wisdom he gathered as he grew old,
There was no way he could ever have told
What fragments, what remnants would be passed on down
For us to keep when he was gone.

Remembering John Romanyshyn

"...and not, when I come to die discover that I had not lived."
—Henry David Thoreau

We used to play old fiddle tunes;
On lazy summer afternoons.
We'd leave the labor to the ants
And play to make the hayfields dance;
Like grasshoppers grown wild and wise
We'd then sit back and socialize.

So thus I came to know a man
Who always seemed to understand
That each day brings a gift of light
And on each clear, star scattered night
Every gleaming, ancient ray
Is a gift sent from the Milky Way.

His eyes were mild; what lay behind
Gleamed with the power of a mind
That sought to make some kind of sense
Of men's delight in violence,
Of human folly and human greed
That takes from others what others need.

At the passing of a man,
We remember what we can;
A learned man of study and thought,
All his life he wrote and taught—
Now a good, wise man is gone

The Day My Father Climbed to Heaven

In the earliest scene I remember
At the start of my memory,
I'm watching my father as he chops down
An old wild cherry tree.

He kept his ax sharp as the sunlight;
It sunk in deep when he swung,
And scattered smooth, clean-scented chips
Like notes that the axe had sung.

I crawled about and gathered the chips
To understand what they were;
There was a ship, and here was a princess
And a knight who fought for her,

And I learned from them their brave story
And sang it as soft as I could,
Lost in a dream that came to me
As I played with those pieces of wood.

Then as I played in the sunlight
And sang my primitive song,
A crack and a crash and a shout from my father
Told me that something was wrong.

"Well, I'll be damned!" said my father
(A phrase that was new to me),
The wind had twisted the cherry's fall;
It was caught in a big maple tree.

My father came over to where I was
And gave me his hat and his shirt;
"Stay right here and mind these things;
Don't want you getting hurt."

He went to the cherry tree, slanting
To the tangled branches above,
And put his hands to the scaly black bark
And gave a great heave and a shove

And nothing happened. He tried again
And again, one more time,
And then he shrugged and hitched up his pants
And then he started to climb.

He went up that tree like it was a beanstalk,
And the next thing I could see
Was my father up there in green leaves and blue sky
Waving down to me.

Then he started to sway back and forth
And wrenched the tree around,
And suddenly all the branches came free
And he rode the tree down to the ground.

It's a long time now my father's been gone
But I still see in my mind's eye
My heavenly father waving to me
Hallowed by leaves and bright sky.

The Clock My Grandfather Made

Before I could talk, my grandfather made
    A curious mantel clock
Of walnut he'd saved for thirty years;
    It looks like a blacksmith shop.

The back of the clock opens up like a door;
    There stands the patient smith;
And in his hand is his blacksmith's hammer
    To strike the hours with,

And every hour he nods his head
    And strikes upon the chime
And through the house the familiar sound
    Tells the present time.

My grandfather wrote that he liked to think
    Of how the clock would run
And keep him in our memory
    Long after he was gone,

And now it's been nearly sixty years
    Since my grandfather passed away
And still his blacksmith strikes the hours
    Of every passing day.

For Peter Schumann
On His Seventieth Birthday

Figures that come looming up in dreams
Remembered from some time before our own,
Images that we carry in our genes—
He gives them mortal flesh and mortal bone,
Then finds a way to give each one a chance
To have a job to do, a role to play,
And some are mute and still, some sing and dance
Until the play is done and put away.
Distinct and different, none are quite the same,
Each with its own unique identity,
Yet each one bears the mark from whence it came
That says to all the world, "'Twas Peter made me"
 And if the puppets could but have their way,
 They all would sing to Peter "Happy Birthday".

For Richard Wilbur
On His Eightieth Birthday

He throws plain English to the sky
And when the words come down
He tosses them back up again
And spins them round and round
Till they become a solid wheel
Well-wrought in such a way,
The wheel keeps turning in the air
When the juggler walks away.

Two Buildings

I

The day we raised up Erik's barn,
Big timbers thunked in place
And framed the restless, artless air
Into a structured space.

Each tenon found its mortise
As the heavy mallet swung
And every beam sang with each blow
Old songs the hills have sung.

Or was it the design itself
Was music to our ears
As Pythagoras heard sweet numbers
And Ptolemy heard the spheres?

II

Two clumps of trees in the meadow grow,
Two islands in a grass-green lake;
One is where they used to throw
The stones that threatened blade and rake.
Amid curled ferns in dark, soaked ground
In the farther clump, a spring is found
That feeds a pipe to the house below.
In the nearer isle of trees and shade
(Their height tells how many years have passed
Since someone stooped to spare his blade
And seized a stone and there it cast)
These stones now stand to enclose a space.

With care each stone is fit in place,
Each wall built well and built to last,
    Each stone in its inevitable home
    Like notes in a tune or words in a poem.

Learning to Speak

For my grandson, Colton

You imitate the sounds we make—
"cow" and "rooster", "dog" and "cat",
and come to know that these are words
that go with this and not with that,
and as the sounds become defined
language is forming in your mind.

Soon the words will start to join
Like little links of verbal chain
And in their combinations shape
New understanding in your brain
Of all that can be held in thought,
Of what is real and what is not.

Now in your play you can pretend;
You offer us an empty cup
And laugh when we so carefully
Tip it to drink nothing up—
Imagination is the key
To mastering reality.

Love

Old Love

Old lovers now, we know each other well.
Our minds have merged; we seldom think alone;
There often seems but little need to tell
An idle thought, for it could be your own.
You are a presence in my mind, as I,
I know quite well, am always there in yours;
To each unspoken question, you reply
And then the thought, no longer mine, is ours.
And we've made love a thousand times and more
On rainy morns or sunny afternoons;
When we lie down, we know well what's in store
And play desires like familiar tunes.
    Although these things are all entirely true,
    Every time you smile, then love is new.

Love and Fire

Passion kindles by friction's heat
Insubstantial fuel
To blaze with sudden flaring light—
Such fires can quickly cool,
Unless well-seasoned, solid sticks
Are shrewdly placed with care
So that the fragile flames may feed,
Not die from lack of air,
And then there are the heavy logs
That slowly burn to embers,
Giving long and steady heat—
So old love remembers.

Our Years

How many times had this huge earth swung 'round
The sun before we met? And then how long
Will it spin on when we are in the ground,
Gone like dreams or long-forgotten songs?
Of all the countless years that have gone by,
Of all the unglimpsed years that yet shall be,
Ours are but few, a blinking of an eye
That gazes over wide eternity.
So let us love each other while we may
And let our hearts be filled with quiet ease
And each and every slowly passing day
Be filled with sunlit, cherished memories.
    Thus though our years remaining be but few,
    We will have done the best that we can do.

Lindsay's Birthday

Oh, do not say that you are growing old
Because once more around the steadfast sun
Again our round and whirling world has rolled
Until at last another orbit's done.
Time lays a heavy hand on bitter souls
Who rail and carp against the world too much;
For those whose all-embracing love unfolds
Their world, Time keeps his lightest touch.
So do not say that you are growing old
Or fear the passing of the stars, far-flung;
The truest words that ever can be told
Are these—it's love that keeps you ever young.

Thus you shall all Time's weary woes repel
By loving well and being loved as well.

A Valentine (2004)

Did fiery stars ignite our love?
Cold planets plan desire?
Did all the turning sky above
Upon our fate conspire?

Or was it all an accident
That led to our first glance
In a universe indifferent
Where worlds collide by chance?

No matter now if by design
Or random happenstance,
I am yours and you are mine
For all this mortal dance.

While You're Away

It's true the birds still sing while you're away,
Clamoring each morning from the trees
About the house, and in their usual way
They flock down to the porch to scatter seeds.
It's true the fire burns with merry flame,
Keeping this old house warm despite the wind,
And through the night the embers do the same
Until at dawn I fill the stove again,
And still the sun keeps rising in the East
And still descends behind the westward hill,
Not noticing your absence in the least
And like as not, it probably never will,

    But every time I softly say your name
    I look around, and nothing is the same.

Happiness

New lovers now no longer young know well
The subtle ways delight decays to pain
And vinegar subsides from spoiled champagne
As quickly as from cheapest muscatel.
We who have suffered from love's careless spell
Are well forewarned and cannot well complain
When smiles droop down to sneers of chill disdain
And passion seeks a newer clientele.

But let us in our ardor persevere
And trust our joy to evermore endure
Without the blight of jealousy or fear
Or doubt, or feeling lost and insecure,
For happiness need never go away
As stars are always there in brightest day.

A Valentine

You are so lovely and so dear to me
That I could wish I were some unseen bird
To perch and sing, nearby where you might be,
Warbling love without a single word.
I would become a book of poetry,
Old and leather bound, to bring to mind
Images from love's sweet memory.
Or I might wish to be a soft, gray cat,
Lithe and nimble, dancing at your feet,
Tumbling like a supple acrobat,
Then posturing with vast feline conceit.
     Such fancies come to mind, for I can't see
     Why you would want to love a man like me.

Words for the Ghost

"I long to talke with some old lover's ghost
Who dyed before the god of Love was borne"

—John Donne, <u>Love's Deitie</u>

Loud love requires tragedy
To burn with hottest fire,
Its fuel imagined ecstasy
And unfulfilled desire.

When they're apart, then lovers long
To touch while passion rages;
They breathe soft feelings forth in song
And write on crumpled pages,

But when at last they can unite
Their limbs in tangled riot,
Then everything is soon all right
And love is calm and quiet.

A long love needs no tragedy
To fuel its steady fire;
It burns with daily ecstasy
And gratified desire.

Falling Dream

She stands, windblown and tall, at the cliff's edge;
Her back is to a common field with shrouds
Of mist, old junipers, and outcropped ledge—
Beyond, only clouds and mountains like clouds.
She leans outward, pressing against a gust
Of wind that blows her hair and blows her clothes,
At ease, as if she knows that she can trust
The air to hold her as it holds the crows
That soar so far below her feet. And now
She turns and beckons me; I come up near,
She firmly takes my hand to show me how
To fly—the earth tugs downward at my fear.
    We step off from the rock to live or die—
    Beyond us is the endless, turning sky.

Had You Been Called

Had you been called as Death's reluctant bride,
Whatever I might have done to hold you back
Would have been no use. Oh, had you died,
The sun then would have risen robed in black
And in the meadows where the bobolink
Had swayed and sung upon the bending weed,
No flowers would have blossomed there, I think,
But only worthless burdock, gone to seed.
But then I saw you smile and felt your hand
Tug my thick gray beard and knew that we
Have still a while to walk across the land
And hear the bobolink and bumblebee
    And hold each other in the summer sun
    And hold each other when the day is done.

Unequal Tender

True love is never to be bought or sold;
No one argues there, I think, and yet
The common barter system seems as cold,
Where love must be with equal measure met.
These market lovers seek imbalanced trade,
That they may gain a greater love for less,
As if their love were something measured, weighed,
And profit the surest way to happiness.
But maybe love is measureless and free,
Never to be exchanged, but only given
Without regard for reciprocity,
Or whether the amounts of love are even.
  Free as Summer sun and soft Spring rain,
  Love loves not just to be loved again.

Old Poems

And I have turned the yellowed, brittle page
To find again an old, familiar phrase
And learn how poets of another age
Would woo and win with polished words of praise
In verses formed as fine as ivory combs,
Would mourn that beauty fades into the tomb,
But promise immortality in poems
That should endure until the dawn of doom.
For I have greatest need of eloquence;
Gray is my beard; near empty is my purse,
Nor may I boast of great accomplishments
Except, perhaps, my modest skill with verse;
    Thus read my lines with a forgiving heart—
    To win your love, I have no other art.

March

My every thought is not always of you—
The shifting gleam of early morning light
Upon old snow, the Winter's residue;
The soaring raven's playful, tricky flight,
The otter tracks beside the thawing stream,
The new Spring calls of chickadee and jay,
Distract me, and for moments it may seem
As if I might not think of you all day,
But then, as when the gusting wind dies down
And lets the pool lie still, sunlit and clear,
The worn stones that were never really gone
Beneath the water suddenly appear,
    So you are always there beneath my thoughts,
    A constant presence that your love has wrought.

The Pumpkin Plot

Each spring I plant my pumpkins
Up where the garden lies;
Maybe this year I'll find a girl
Who'll make me pumpkin pies.

Six hills I plant, and that's a lot
Of vines, you may surmise,
But you need lots of pumpkins
To have lots of pumpkin pies.

On summer's evenings I weed them well
Amongst the fireflies
And dream of a lovely lady
Making pumpkin pies.

By August the pumpkins start to grow
And some are quite nice size
But I've not yet found a woman
Who'll make me pumpkin pies.

When I take my pumpkins to the fair
I expect to win first prize,
And maybe meet a lady
Who longs to make pumpkin pies.

When all the hills are red and gold,
A pleasure to the eyes,
I harvest lots of pumpkins
For lots of pumpkin pies.

I store them upstairs in the eaves
Where it is cool and dry
And wonder where the woman is
Who makes good pumpkin pie.

Come Valentine's Day, they start to rot
And I must realize
This year has been another year
When there's no pumpkin pie.

But when it's time to order seeds
My hopes soar to the skies,
And I order lots of pumpkin seed
For lots of pumpkin pies.

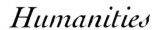

Humanities

Metaphor

In a linguistic magic trick
The thing becomes something it's not
By power latent in the words,
Whether spoken or in shifting thought.
But in the poet's verbal sleight,
Unlike the street magician's ploy,
There is a purpose to the trick;
A metaphor is not a toy.
Although the dictionary gives
Meanings succinctly accurate
For half a million words or more,
Feeling and thought are infinite,
Unspeakable unless transformed.
As Aztecs trapped their gods in jaguars,
And lucid, clear-eyed Greeks once caught
Their dreams in flimsy nets of stars.

Worlds

My father said that in the day
The stars just *seem* to go away;
Although the sun obscures their light,
They shine by day as in the night.

One day I lay upon my back
In an empty hearth on stones burned black;
When I looked up the chimney, I could see
One small star shining down on me.

The nighttime sky is bright with stars
Yet what we see isn't all there are;
Beyond the stars that we can see
Lie countless sweeps of galaxies,

And out beyond those galaxies
Worlds in vast varieties
Continue far out past the brink
Of what the mortal mind can think.

Yet with the coming of the dawn
The starlight dwindles and then is gone;
But for some clouds, the sky seems bare,
Although we know the stars are there.

When the morning lies unfurled,
I turn once more to my own small world,
Forget the far-flung stars of night
And strive to get some small thing right.

While overhead, the Pleiades
And stars in endless, swirling seas
Of galaxies and nebulae
Drift unseen by mortal eyes.

Visibility

When the sun outshines the stars
Then we see this world of ours;
When the stars shine bright and clear,
The universe can then appear.

In Adversity

Trust the world—it will never fail you;
Take strength from the great migrations of geese,
Of salmon, hummingbirds and caribou
In their determined journeys, and the peace
Of grubs that wrap themselves in sleep and dream
Enormous, fragile wings; likewise the bright
Certainty of weeds that thrust and scheme
Their way through asphalt to the living light.
Take strength and share the pulsing force
That moves all creatures slowly towards the light,
That moves your mind still closer to the source
Of thought, that makes an eye before there's sight.
     Trust the world—it will never fail you;
     Trust what this world is slowly coming to.

Spectrum

That afternoon it felt like fall.
The angled light was hard and clean;
Where shadows fell the air was cold
Although the garden still was green.

From the southwest came a squall;
By gusting winds the trees were blown
And bright, clear rain fell on the hills
Yet through it all the sun still shone.

Then suddenly the wind died down
And as I watched and all was still
The light broke through the falling rain
And arced above the eastward hill.

They say that pilots in their planes
See rainbows as a perfect wheel;
This wheel was sunk into the ground
Half-buried in the upper field,

Or so at least I let it seem.
It is the way of idle eyes
To speculate in idle dreams
On what the world we know implies.

Eyes

The tender rabbit's eyes are placed
So warily wide-spread
That he sees all the way around
With the least turn of his head.

The fox's canny eyes are set
Much further to the front
To guide his jaws where they must close
At the ending of his hunt.

Man's close-set eyes are placed to judge
The distance to a limb:
Back when he lived in trees that was
What mattered most to him.

Thus always more than half the world
Evades our forward stare,
And what may lurk behind our backs?
We never know what's there.

If there a grinning dancer stands
And should we quickly spin,
He'll leap around to stand unseen
While we see where he's been.

Crows and Humanity

They say a crow has been observed
Bending a slender piece of wire
To make a hook for getting food—
Next thing we know they'll master fire.
How we may differ from other species
Has always been a major question;
We've always sought some great distinction
From the common pack and herd.
Once we thought we had a soul
And that we had received the Word
But such notions were finally found
To stand on unsubstantial ground.
We thought then reason and making tools
Were what made us truly special
But now a crow has shown what fools
We were to hold to such insanity—
There's nothing unique about humanity.
(This is not a great calamity.)

Kaleidoscope

Tiny bits of colored glass
Tumble in an aimless mass,
Then the light that passes through
Is distorted in our view.
The pretty patterns that we see
Of glowing, perfect symmetry
Are no less fair,
Although not there.

Purpose

When I was young I wrote for love;
To catch the girls who caught my eye
I cast my lines with pretty rhymes
And waited for a soft reply.

Now that I'm old, I write no more
For young girls, lovely as the dawn;
I put words where I think they'll stay
A little while when I am gone.

Preaching to the Birds

"You must hear the bird's song without attempting
to render it into nouns and verbs."

—Ralph Waldo Emerson

Crows came flapping down to perch
Among the shining olive leaves;
Doves came nodding to his church
As sparrows fluttered at his sleeves.

St. Francis then preached to the birds,
Mimicking their songs to make new speech.
Warbling his newfound words,
What then did the good saint preach?

What teaching could the saint present
When they were gathered at his call?
How could they learn what "savior" meant
Who never sinned and will not fall?

Nor need they knowledge of His grace
Whose wings ascend to brush His face.

For Benjamin Franklin: On receiving his honorary doctorate from the University of Saint Andrews, Edinburgh, Scotland, 1759

"Nature and Nature's Laws lay hid in night;
God said 'Let Newton be' and all was light."

—Alexander Pope

When I was ten and had to leave my school,
Then I resolved to live by Reason's Rule.
I sought to discipline my willful mind
And studied every book that I could find,
And when I found an author writing well,
Then I would write an essay parallel,
So that by imitation of my betters,
I came to have some modest skill with letters.

Each evening with the setting of the sun,
I asked myself what good I might have done;
When I could see some small accomplishment,
Then I would say that day had been well spent.
I did this, not because God said I should;
Reason alone will lead one to do good.
If God in fact designed a Master Plan,
Still he leaves the management to man;
Seldom does He deign to glance below
And Reason tells us all that we can know.
God let Newton be, the poet said,
And I but followed on where Newton led.
Therefore I utilized plain common sense

To frame my questions in experiments
And then observed how the results combine
To reveal the Laws of Nature's Grand Design.
From those known laws, one may then deduce
Broad application for the general use
And benefit of all, as we in turn
Benefit by those from whom we learn.

Although I've seldom been a classroom student,
I have loved learning and never was truant
From the wide, wide world, wherein I sought
To study well whatever nature taught.
What I thus learned was what in time allowed
My hand to draw forth lightning from the cloud.
Henceforth, having been honored by degrees
I shall be Doctor Franklin, if you please,
A title that I shall most proudly bear
Without, one hopes, becoming doctrinaire.

Sword Swallower

Like a gawky nestling, he tips his head
Far back and stretches wide his gaping jaws,
And slowly the glittering, fearsome blade is fed
Downward, to the clatter of our applause.
Then, the hilt against his teeth, he stands
Exalted, his arms flung skyward as if to give
Welcome to some god whose great, gnarled hands
Could draw the offered blade and let him live.
After we applaud, we watch him take
The sword back out. Exhaling our relief
That this time there was no obscene mistake,
We cheer again; anxiety was brief.

      Although no god came down to steal the scene,
      We felt a presence, a rustle behind the screen.

After All

"In History I always was the dunce,"
She says and laughs a little at the thought,
"Perhaps I might have learned about it once,
but History was hard and badly taught,
and after all, I mean for heaven's sake,
who cares about just who did what and when—
I'd like to know what difference can it make
If we forget what happened way back then?"

And so the past becomes a jumbled blur
Of faces on a coin or dollar bill;
The words of Lincoln mean no more to her
Than what Spinoza said about free will.

Of what has ever been or yet will be,
The little we can know is history.

A Priest with the Conquistadors Considers the Native Peoples

It seems most likely that they are much the same
As we are in their basic wants and needs;
They eat much fish and various sorts of game
And know enough to gather and plant seeds
Of corn and squash and beans. I cannot say
If they in fact have souls as Christians do;
Although some theologians say they may,
It hardly seems as if that could be true.
Yet in many ways they seem to be
Quite human—they take delight in war
And torture prisoners ingeniously
Then burn them at the stake, all dark with gore.
    What I will say I find to be most odd—
    They fail to do this in the name of God.

Petrarch's Futility

No language can express the pounding heart;
Even those whose craft is well-wrought speech
Can't hammer out linked chains of words that reach
Around what's felt within. There is no art
To grope and grasp and bring forth more than part
Of all the pain and ecstasy that each
Poor, battered soul contains. No book can teach
Language to express the pounding heart.

But even if there were some way to say
The endless, hopeless love that blazed within
For fourteen thousand days and nights and more,
Why would she want to hear his words portray
A futile love? Better had he been
A flat gray stone to lay before her door.

Memento Mori

They say that scholars used to place
A skull upon the desk in case
They might forget that pulse and breath
So soon will stop—"Remember Death,"
The silent skull would seem to say,
"Then know the savor of each day."

And sometimes with my hand I trace
The bones that lie beneath my face,
And then my fingers seem to see
My own skull staring back at me.
That stranger there beneath my skin
Gives good counsel from within,
Saying what bones always say—
"Know the savor of each day."

Necessity

Once begun, the well-told tale
Comes to life and makes demands;
What will happen in the story
Is not in the teller's hands.

The child, unwanted, cast adrift
On stormy waters, must be found
And brought up, then go home again—
Such a child cannot be drowned.
The king who, for whatever reason,
Becomes a beggar in disguise
Must be skilled enough to fool
Even the most suspicious eyes.
Also, such a beggar king
Can't beg forever from town to town;
He has his moment when he must rise
And resume his royal robes and crown.
The halves of the ring that lovers break
Between them as their secret sign
Are inexorably drawn together
By the power of the tale's design;
Like fragments of a shattered soul,
They cannot rest till they are whole.

But lover, child, or beggar king
Can never know what we can tell,
Else the story would be spoiled—
Break the plot and break the spell.

In the world we live in, though,
There are no patterns we can see;
Things fall together or apart
By chance and not necessity.
If in some way our random lives
Make a kind of cosmic sense,
Such could only be discerned
By more than mortal intelligence.

Modesty

There is a roughness to the human eye
That gives a worn, unfocused look to things
In public view, as if abraded by
The public gaze. In deep-woods wanderings
One sees the twirling, graceful leaf alight
To float upon its image in a stream,
Or finds odd mushrooms risen overnight—
Such shy and fragile visions somehow seem
More well defined than pigeons at the feet
Of statues dozing in the public's stare
Or sparrows fluttering along a street
That seem to flutter in a thicker air.
    When things are looked at by too many eyes,
    They blur and merge and fade, like oft-told lies.

Finding One's Way

As we went out for an evening walk
At the end of a long, rainy day,
A night crawler squirmed in the wet black road.
It seemed to have lost its way,

But then it headed straight over the road
Toward the weeds at the edge of the tar,
Suddenly, sure as a man far at sea
When the clouds part below the North Star.

The asphalt was bleak, empty and endless
In two ways the worm might have gone,
But although it was blind, it knew where to go;
Something had guided it on.

Clouds

"Do you see yonder cloud that's almost in the shape of a camel?"
—<u>Hamlet</u>

White puffs of cloud are scattered now
Across the deep blue of July,
Idle vapors in thin air
Without intent to signify,
But as I watch the summer wind
Change the shape of every cloud,
I look for forms I recognize;
Faces and strange, vague creatures crowd
Across the theater of the skies.

Still the mythic impulse runs
Deep within the mortal mind
To animate an indifferent world
With figures of our mortal kind.

Leaving

She wanted a clean passing,
A simple end to breath.
As the end drew near, she carefully planned
The arrangements of her death.

She sorted out her papers,
Discarding each old, paid bill,
And wrote down things we should know about
Each possession in her will.

And then she cleaned the closets,
And emptied the desk drawer,
And then cleaned out the attic
That had never been cleaned before.

But what she finally left behind
Was more than she could have known,
As the still air holds a presence
When a small brown bird has flown.

Cosmos

I went once to the house of one whose mind
Had broken long before she'd finally died.
All that kept her going was her pride;
She lived for years alone and nearly blind
In a small world her madness had designed.
In delicate arrangements, she had tried
With twigs and string and eggshells to provide
For some strange fate her madness had divined.

The mice that knew no other world well might
Have thought (suppose they were intelligent)
That all was in accordance with hard laws
To be hypothesized and proven right.
The proof they could not find, they would invent;
Intelligence demands there be a cause.

Janus

Children love a doorway—they will stand
For hours it seems, door flung open wide,
Oblivious to draft or reprimand,
Pleased to be not in nor yet outside,
But rather so precisely in between
There's not the least suggestion of intent
To go or come; thus they achieve the mean
Unconsciously, not knowing what is meant.
In the ever-changing world of youth,
The meanings of these thresholds shift and fade,
Elusive as deceptive dreams of truth
Dreamt in summer's long and dappled shade;
    Let children keep the doorway while they may,
    To find their balance, before they go away.

On the Library Steps

Men used to heat the public baths, they say,
By burning in the name of Christ those scrolls
That held the thoughtful light of Grecian day,
Bathing their bodies as they cleansed their souls.
And for a thousand plodding years or so
The light seemed thicker and the darkness masked
The once well-trodden ways of how to know
Or how a question might be truly asked.
Then once again arose the honest light
And men began to think as we still do;
To reason became once more a common right
And anyone could know what Euclid knew.
    Now torches waver toward the library door,
    Borne by the well meaning, as before.

Wings

When ponderous lizards first began
To walk and wander everywhere,
What wings were then the first to fan
The planet's pristine, steamy air?
What leathern folds like hell-born sails
Spread upon long, hollow bones,
Tipped with curved, keen-pointed nails,
Flapped and floundered there alone?
What reptilian untried brain
Piloted that clumsy glide?
As primal wings held firm to plane,
What mind then acted as their guide?
What sultry wind blew then to train
Those wings to arc and slowly ride?
And after rising to the skies,
What mind looked down through hooded eyes?

Such was the first-born earthly wing;
No feathers, pure and soft and white
With soft angelic flutterings
Flew forth from out that primal night.

Angel wings could never grow
And still leave arms to work on things;
Man made a choice back long ago
To make his way with arms, not wings.

The Best and the Worst

"The best lack all conviction while the worst are
filled with passionate intensity."
> —Yeats, "The Second Coming"

Yeats thought that he'd described our time
When passion justifies each crime
While honest men stand idly by
And vacillate, and wonder why
Others bomb and rape and kill
And none can stop them, or none will.

But far more dreadful is our age
When all our best are filled with rage
That clouds each noble, decent mind
And leaves all common sense behind;
In God's or Right's or Freedom's name,
The best and worst now think the same.

Politics

There are those among us who are wise,
Who see what will result from foolish acts,
Who look upon the truth with steady eyes,
And examine well what seem to be the facts.
Far more are fools, with minds controlled by greed,
Who do not know or care to know what's real,
Who follow where each idle whim may lead,
And seldom think, although they strongly feel.
Deafened by their fears, they cannot hear
When wiser voices try to show the way,
And so they watch fake shows and drink poor beer,
And say again the things they always say.
    How such a world can ever better be
    Is the great puzzle of democracy.

Fifes and Drums

They say in Concord when the redcoats came
Their scornful fifes and drums played "Yankee Doodle"
To taunt the locals with a yokel's name
And burn the ears of untrained rural rabble.
They thought themselves an overwhelming threat;
They thought our men would likely break and run
When faced with lines of slender bayonets
Advancing to the rolling of the drums.
We had one fife; we had one drum and played
A tune from times when men defied the crown
On wind-swept Highland ground—"The White Cockade"
To sound across the fields to Concord town.
    The muskets flashed; the redcoats broke and ran;
    The village bells rang out The Rights of Man.

Old Bones

I.

Our kind, for some six million years it seems,
Lived as furtive scavengers, like wild dogs,
Until we were provoked by moon-wrought dreams
To fill our minds with muttered monologues.
And so we mumbled on and watched the stars
Arrange themselves in symbols we could name;
We learned the use of fire and sharp spears;
We felt our souls leap skywards with the flames.
Then fierce cats cowered; gray wolves skulked and fled;
Great shambling beasts with heavy, hairy hides
Kept us warmly clad and kept us fed—
We strode upon the hills like primal gods.
    And when we had no thing to fear but man,
    Then all our endless, savage wars began.

II.

Long ago, slowly, stumbling, we learned
To walk upright and use our unskilled hands
To shape hard stone near where our fires burned,
Then wandered far in harsh and hostile lands.
And soon enough, Troy's towers fell in smoke;
Rough stone was smoothed by Michelangelo,
And when first Newton and then Franklin spoke,
There was no end to what we came to know.
Yet when at last this spinning sphere shall whirl
No more about the dim, exhausted sun,
Then nothing will be left of our bright world

And Time shall cease, with no more years to come.
    What then the point of all the arts of men?
    We think and build and sing because we can.

III.

The evidence of hate endures through time;
We find the ancient skeletons that show
How men were killed when killing was no crime.
The skull, crushed by a harsh, decisive blow,
The spine that holds embedded, sharpened stone,
These tell us that our wars are nothing new.
Hate leaves its record printed in the bone
And bones are hard, and last as hard things do.
Love breaks no bones, though brittle hearts may break
And being broken, come to naught but dust;
Soft vows of passion, such as lovers make,
Last no longer than their mortal lust,
    But since the children of our kind need care,
    That we are here shows us that love was there.

Thanksgiving

Our Pilgrim Fathers long ago
Gave thanks that they were still alive,
That, few and weak, they could survive
The raw, damp winds and drifting snow
That sifted through the endless trees
While at their backs the endless seas
Crashed against the broken coast.
Despite all that their new world cost
In this new world they held their land,
Although they could not understand
The nation latent in their deeds
No more than did the random seeds
Of common European weeds
That soon would claim a continent.
They filled their days with toil and prayer
And never doubted God was there
Or that their works served His intent,
And the long labor of each day
Forged anew their will to stay.

Nigh on four hundred winters' snows
Have fallen on the graves of those
Staunch, sober men in black and gray
Who kept the first Thanksgiving Day.
But though those men are now long gone
We keep alive the dream begun
When first their footsteps marked our sand
In a hard time, in a hard land.

From the Homeric World

A Girl Reading _The Iliad_

The slanting sun haloes her well-brushed hair
While in a tangled, thoughtless schoolgirl sprawl
She broods upon <u>The Iliad</u>. What she reads there
Seems nearly as absurd to her as all
The hormone-roiled, half-mad young men she knows.
While Homer's warriors, with arrogant swords and spears,
Go down to feed gaunt dogs and harsh-beaked crows.
In her mind another scene appears;
Those hard Achaians have become the men
She studies in the ads in _Rolling Stone,_
Whose god-like, empty eyes caress her when
She lies upon her doll-strewn bed alone,
Dreaming of the bright glory she has learned,
How for her sake a city could be burned.

Homer

I did not make the song of Ilion;
The goddess filled my lungs and shaped my breath
To sing of Helen, fathered by a swan
Who brought to Troy sharp bronze and looming death.
No light came through my blank and stony eyes,
My thoughts were shadows, moving on a wall,
Of men like gods and gods in men's disguise—
The smoke of funeral pyres was over all.
As breakers surge up from the wind-lashed sea
To seethe upon a broken, rocky shore,
Waves of language billowed over me
And I sang the epic of the Trojan War;
    The words I cast like thistle on the wind
    Took root to flourish in the minds of men.

Cassandra

Apollo saw me naked and I fled;
He followed me and placed his blazing hand
Where the braids lay coiled upon my head.
Then visions that I could not understand
Of burning cities, butchered kings and queens
Swirled like altar-smoke before my eyes.
I had to tell the things that I had seen.
When none believed what I would prophesy,
I thought it was an angry god who made
Those whom I warned so certain that I lied.
I stood alone; I felt I'd been betrayed,
But any who have told the truth, or tried,

> Have learned how truth evades the mortal ear;
> What men expect to hear is all they hear.

Courage

"I have learned to be valiant, and to fight
always in the foremost ranks."

—Hector in <u>The Iliad</u>

A kind of manly courage can be learned—
Although great Hector knew that Troy would fall,
His wife be taken slave, his city burned,
He still was brave enough to put it all
Out of his mind when he went forth to fight,
Doomed by his very armor and the gods;
Defending a cause he knew was less than right,
He did not pause to estimate the odds.
But women's courage seems to be untaught,
So fearlessly they give their love to men,
Freely, as if no response were sought,
Loving not only to be loved again.
     Such gentle loving seems more brave by far
     Than any reckless murdering in war.

Honor

I know this world is far from what we might
Choose if it were ours to make anew.
Millions stray in darkness, lacking the light
Of wisdom's flame that flickers but burns true.
Lies and greed are principles of State;
Religion is the mob's hysteric chant;
Decency is overcome by hate;
Truth would speak out but mostly, sadly, can't.
Yet still we must admit the faithful sun
Keeps its appointed schedule in the sky;
Deer feed in mountain meadows, while salmon spawn
Ecstatically in cold, clear streams nearby;
Small, bright birds have praise for every dawn,
  And some men still stand as their fathers stood
  When honor's pipes and drums beat in their blood.

Prayer

Great Achilles chose to die
That he might have eternal fame;
Three thousand years have since passed by
And still today we know his name.

When the rash king hurt his pride
He quit, and prayed the Greeks would lose.
The gods agreed, Greeks fell and died,
What happened next he did not choose.

His best friend pitied those who died,
And fought to keep tall Hector back;
When he went down, Achilles cried
And took his huge spear from the rack.

Grieving, to avenge his friend
He dragged tall Hector in the dust;
Though he was honored, in the end,
The gods are cruel when they are just.

Penelope

Through the warp the heddles held and spread,
Thread from the shifting shuttle turned into
New cloth that filled the loom, moving ahead
Steadily as the intricate pattern grew.
Then, in the long night's stillness, weary, she
Reduced the fabric down to strands again.
When morning stopped that work, Penelope
Began anew to dupe the sodden men.

Thus the years like wooden wheels rolled past,
Rumbling with the loss of youth and hope,
But she was shrewd and true as a ship's mast
That sings with well-filled sails and taut, pitched rope,

Deep and shifting as the wine-dark sea,
The moon-drawn power of her subtlety.

Odysseus at Ninety
Remembers the Princess Nausicäa

I'll tell you this—none of it was easy;
Wisdom is no light burden for a man—
The endless, muttered counsel of the dead,
Always urging caution, yet insisting,
"Take it! Now! Before the light is gone."
And the immortal women—
Haunting, lovely as deep blue-water dreams,
But though their bodies sang beneath my hand
Like taut lines at the onset of the wind,
Always they remained beyond my grasp,
And the mortal girl I could have truly held
Forever would have held me in her land.
This is how it was.

Long years ago I rose at dawning light—
An unknown beach, the roaring, crashing surf,
The searching cries of clamorous, wheeling gulls,
The salt crust itching at my sea-soaked hide—
And there she stood…

What makes some women so entirely lovely?
Do not all faces have the same components—
Two eyes, nose in the middle, mouth below?
Yet I've seen some so subtly composed,
Softly lucent as slow mid-summer moons,
They tugged into confusion a man's life-blood,
As the moon disturbs the surging of the sea.

When we took Helen from the blazing city,
Her eyes wide with terror, her delicate knees
Smudged with soot, her regal robe all torn
And scorched with wind-blown sparks, her fabled beauty
Struck each man like an arrow in the lungs.

Ah, but here an aging man digresses.
Nausicäa, the princess on the beach—
I see her radiant in the morning light,
Her wind-blown garments pressed against her body,
And I, who had been welcome in the beds
Of women who were not of mortal flesh,
Could find a promise of what all men seek
In clear young eyes that said she longed to know
All that women come to know, and more.

What kept me from her, willing as she was?
A wind-blown shadow of high destiny?
Even then, my life was not my own;
My loves, my wars, my voyagings became
The common stuff of epics of our race,
Chanted near the hearths of famous kings,
And to become the legend and the song,
I left behind all else I might have been.

I felt her eyes on me when I embarked,
And when I knew she could no longer see
The sails that sang above me in the wind,
I drew my cloak about my face and wept.

So I left her in that far-off land
To come back here and slay a hundred men,
Take back my throne and noble, faithful queen
And by example teach to smaller men
A way to breathe more deeply in a world
Unmagical, yet perfect in its way.

Still, evenings when I watch the shifting sea
Change colors in the fading, rose-tinged light
I drink a little raw, dark, unmixed wine
And see her still as she was then, immortal
In my memory...
And from afar I hear the sirens singing
Wild songs of half-forgotten memories
And dreams that haunt the twilight of the mind.

Zeus

Not even I could tell what wars would come
From taking Leda to my feathered breast;
Glory blazed across the sky for some
And piercing, choking death came to the rest.
Leda told her daughter all she'd learned
Of love beneath the arc of my wide wing.
Then Helen drove men mad, a city burned,
And a goddess taught a blind man how to sing.
But had I known, I'd still have done the same.
As she lay beside the dark, swift-running stream,
Her body burning with its mortal flame,
The shadow of a swan swept through her dream.
    Although no mortal flame can burn for long,
    The smoke of Ilion swirls through the blind man's song.

Diomedes Speaks of Fame

Achilles?
I never understood the man at all.
Thetis, his mother, goddess of the sea,
Could not have told him, immortal as she was,
How sweet the sunlight and the air become
To one who knows that death is bleak and dull,
And so she let him choose, without advice,
Between two destinies. He could have lived
A long and easy life; a king ruling
An easy, fertile land, and in his age
Death would come upon him in his sleep
As soft as some white-clouded summer dream,
But he was young—the youngest of us all—
Although he'd seen enough good men go down,
Still he chose dying young for fame
And soon enough his blood was slowly soaking
The hard-packed, trampled plain of Ilion.

I watched the pyre where his body burned,
And as I cut my hair to mourn his passing,
I felt the sunlight on my lifted face.

My business in the battle was to stay
Alive while others who stood against me died.
War was what I knew—I was a soldier,
No more, no less. Whatever fame might come
My way was never really my concern,
Although I liked to listen to Chrysies
When she would lie beside me after love

And lightly run her nails across my chest
And talk of how the art of prophecy
Was in her blood. She'd smile and twist her hair
And tell of how great bards would sing our story
After generations of men had come
And vanished from the green and sunlit world.
On an island in the River Ocean
Where the Great Bear circles far above the sea,
Men would shape their mouths to countless words,
Whirling in the wind like yellow leaves,
And thus could say the things that she could not
About the shifting tides of subtle feelings
She knew beneath my scarred and heavy hands.
Perhaps. But stories flow like mountain waters
Finding shape in rivers to the sea.
Who knows how a man may be remembered
By those whose fathers' fathers are not yet born,
Or how the truth of what we knew at Troy
May change in songs sung far across the seas
In language not yet spoken, not yet dreamed.

What I have is good enough for me.
I feel the wind and sun upon my skin
And know, whatever may be yet to come,
I fought with gods like men and men like gods.

Circe

When on Aiaia's rocks I stand and watch
The sunlight dancing on the singing sea
I think of how I too was born like sparks,
Like the morning mist drawn by the sun
From the water, for when great Ocean's daughter
Submitted to the strong need of the sun,
Then I was engendered.

Here on this remote and hallowed isle,
I lived alone, with naught for company
But wide-browed wolves and long-maned, tawny cats
Which honored me but could not share my thoughts
Or join me in my splendid, empty bed.
And when men came, they looked upon my beasts
And me with widened eyes wherein I saw
Their fear, their lust, that made them bestial;
I treated them as the beasts that they had to be,
And penned them up with others of their kind.

And so the stars in their configurations
That mortals see as pictures of the gods
Arose up out of Ocean's vast gray waters
And sank again into the western sea.
I knew some day a man would come to me
Whose mind would leap like sunlight on the surf,
So lucid that no charm or murmured spell
Could swirl the steady current of his thought.

So when Odysseus stood there in my hall
And scorned my magic with his mocking eyes
And held his battered sword up to my throat,
My body trembled like thin bronze cymbals clashed
Before some savage king; my knees dissolved
And I knelt before his calloused, sandaled feet.
I swore to hence forego my hard-won craft,
My magic and my tightly-woven spells,
For I knew well I still possessed the charm
To make him take me in his sinewy arms
And bear my yielding body to the bed.
And so the stars moved round the turning sky:
Twelve times the full moon's path was on the sea
While he forgot his troubled island home,
His aging, time-worn wife, and all that world
Where nothing can endure.

Although I never thought that he would tire
Of my immortal body or my mind,
He said that he must leave. Right then I might
Have told him all—the perils of his voyaging,
The menace of the men who sought his wife
And throne, but would that wary man believe
I spoke hard truth, not lies to keep him here?
No, I sent him to Tiresias
Among the flickering shadows of the dead
And thought perhaps that he might choose to stay.

When he sailed for home, I might have used
My art to know if he survived the sea
And sharp bronze blades awaiting him at home,
But when I watched his black ship merge
With the gray sea-fog, I let him go
Into the mists of memory.

That was long ago.
But still sometimes I cannot help but wonder
If he remembered me before he died
And longed for one whose thoughts flashed like light
On rippled water, and moved like soft gray mist
Upon the moon-drawn tide.

978-0-595-35990-5
0-595-35990-6

Printed in the United States
55893LVS00006B/322-372

9 780595 359905